Clarity Mapping

A

Guided Journal

to Living an

Intentional Life

Clarity Mapping

Ashley LeMieux

HarperOne
An Imprint of HarperCollins*Publishers*

HarperCollins books may be purchased for educational, business, or sales promotional use. For information, please email the Special Markets Department at SPsales@harpercollins.com.

FIRST EDITION

Art © Shutterstock, Inc.

Library of Congress Cataloging-in-Publication Data has been applied for.

ISBN 978-0-06-302785-5

22 23 24 25 26   LSC   10 9 8 7 6 5 4 3 2 1

To Alex, Summer, and JJ—for all the love you bring to my life

Contents

Finding The Clarity That Leads To Freedom

Are you the type of person for whom everything just falls perfectly into place? Your path to your career and family life has been seamless and fulfilling, life hasn't thrown you many surprises, and everything feels simple and easy? No? Me either. Welcome to the club of hard knocks. It's less lonely here than you think.

When life doesn't go the way we think it will, or the way we wanted it to, it's easy to get stuck. And when we're stuck, it's overwhelming to know where to start to get moving again. What I shared in my latest book, *I Am Here*, is all about how I learned that finding clarity in your life doesn't have to happen in the faraway future. It can happen right here, right now.

I believe this because the moments in my life that I thought were absolutely going to break me are also the same moments that have led me here today! Let me start by telling you about one of the most confusing moments in my life. I was lying on an oversized bed in a fancy hotel room that someone else was paying for (okay, Ashley, real hard . . . what's wrong with you?), in the middle of a city I had always dreamed of going to. I had just finished speaking alongside bestselling authors that only in my wildest dreams did I ever think I would be sharing a stage with. Sounds great, right? I always imagined that in achieving these dreams, there would be a feeling of arrival, of joy, of freedom, and of the main thing I was missing in my life: peace. But there wasn't.

Instead, throughout that day, I had been putting out fires at my company. My husband and I had also just lost the two children we had permanent guardianship of during an unexpected contested adoption, after raising them for four years, and every dream that I once had was now crumbling around me (you can read more about this part of my life in my first book, *Born to Shine*). It was like one of those nightmares where you try to scream for help but no words come out, and you try to run but your legs are cemented into the pavement, and so you just sit in fear, watching it all burn to the ground. My life was turning into ashes, and there wasn't a thing I could do to stop it. I didn't know who I was anymore.

Have you ever felt like this? Do you ever feel like in the chaos of life, in the unexpected events, in reaching for dreams, in the balancing and the doubt and the expectations that are on you, that you start forgetting who it is that you actually are? That all around you is the ash and rubble from dreams that have burned?

Maybe right now you're in a place where you have everything you ever thought you wanted. The relationship, the kids, the job, the education . . . whatever that *thing* is that you always told yourself was the end goal, except now you've found it has become the thing that drains you. The thing that makes you wonder who you really are beneath the title.

Or perhaps those things that you've dreamed about for so long and worked so hard for haven't happened yet. And you feel tired, and broken, and confused as to what path you should go down next because nothing seems to be freaking working.

I'm going to tell you a little secret. If life was going to break you, it would have broken you by now. And because it hasn't broken you, it means that you have two options at the moment:

1 Run from your pain.
2 Reclaim your power.

In that hotel room, wondering what to do next, I realized I had already tried running and it didn't work. I didn't know what to do next. I yearned to flip it all around, to choose a path that would be guided by power, clarity, and freedom, so I started staring at myself every day in the mirror, saying things like, "I am a good mother," "I am courageous and brave," "I am full of life," "I am attracting the people in my life I want to be around," "I am open and receptive to all of the good the universe has to offer me." For everything I felt I was lacking, I started declaring that I actually *had* it or *was* it.

Which led to me learning that I had spent so long seeking validation and truth outside of myself that I was missing out on what I actually needed, which was to go inward and start uncovering the woman who had become trapped in a life that she didn't want to be living. I needed to uncover my true self that was buried deep inside.

This is why I'm here with you, now. I want to help you remember, and also discover maybe even for the first time, who you are! When you know who you are, then you can uncover what you can do, who you can be.

How to Use this Book

This workbook was written to read in tandem with *I Am Here*. If you haven't read it yet, that's okay, but it would be even more impactful to read it at the same time you embark on this journey. The work you'll do in these pages will help you nail down what changes in your life would bring you more joy, create a more intentional home life, create a meaningful morning routine, get the courage to apply for a job or quit the one you're at, discover who you are, or give yourself permission to go all in on building a new dream with confidence and excitement. This workbook is for the college girl trying to discover her professional career, the stay-at-home mom who is overwhelmed and losing who she is, the entrepreneur who wants to take things to the next level, and the women who are standing back up and creating a new life after loss.

As you uncover clarity, I hope that you absolutely wreck these pages! Completely cover them in notes, writing, doodles, thoughts, highlights . . . like your own journal. If this workbook is completely unreadable and filled up by the end, then you did it right. I encourage you to tear out the pages that really speak to you and hang them up somewhere you can look at them every day.

We will start by reframing our thoughts, and then embark on an illuminating thirty-day journey that has daily prompts to help you uncover yourself and refocus your time and energy. The prompts are the same prompts that I discovered as I decided to start really living again after digging myself out of one of the lowest points of my life. They will give you clarity and purpose each day, and I am so excited for you to experience whatever comes as a result of creating the morning practice. And since seasons of life change, and we are constantly growing and changing as people, my hope is that the thirty-day journey helps you create an ongoing habit to daily ask yourself these questions and bring clarity no matter where you find your life going.

Next, you will create your own Clarity Map. Perhaps you started doing this work with *I Am Here*—great! I will walk you through two common Clarity Maps: mapping out your personal life and mapping out your professional life. I'll ask questions and give ideas that will help you fill out an actionable Clarity Map. I promise you'll feel empowered as you let go of what is holding you back and identify what it is that you really want in your future.

When we start reimagining our future we can then reclaim our power, which is the final section of this book. You are powerful, even if you don't feel like it all the time. What does reclaiming our power look like? It looks like staying true to yourself and stopping false narratives about who you are that are getting in the way of you being able to fully live freely and purposefully. In the final section, you'll be given guidance and space to create your own mantras and affirmations that will guide you moving forward.

Before we start our journey together, I want to share a few mantras that have really impacted me. A mantra is simply a declaration of truth that helps us remember who we are and not accept anything less. Say them out loud, and when you get to the last one, write down the first thing that comes to your head. This is your starting place.

"I am inviting change and am open to all of the good life has to offer me."

"I am worthy of love."

"I am full of courage."

"I am ready to . . ." (fill in the blank) _____

Have a relationship based in personal and collective growth, to end the chapter that's been long and unending and start life again.

Take a moment to read what you've written down for the last mantra. This will be your guiding principle for the rest of your journey. Deep down, you already know what you need—now it's time to go and get it!

Healing and change don't happen in one moment; it's constant movement. That constant movement can look like having fun or having the hard, necessary conversations about the things that are preventing us from fully moving forward so we can create the change and healing we want in our lives . . . and we can do it together. Creating change and healing our thoughts brings the clarity we're all seeking. Clarity about who we really are. And clarity, my friend, brings freedom. Freedom to live a life you want, as you are. Let's get started.

SECTION ONE

Reframe Your Thoughts

hances are if you picked up this workbook, you're probably look-ing to dive into the goal-setting, life-changing, action-packed work of creating your own Clarity Map and moving on with life. So why are we starting with reframing our thoughts?

What I've found in my own life, and with the women I've worked with, is that sometimes we allow negative thoughts to take up so much of our time and mental energy that we just accept them as truth. In fact, according to one study done by the National Science Foundation, 80 percent of our thoughts are negative, and 95 percent of those thoughts are recurring! No wonder we're so tired every day; we repeatedly beat ourselves down with our thoughts. We need to reframe our thoughts so that who we are can be honored, treasured, and seen! Only once we're clear about who we are and what messages we're telling ourselves can we move forward to accomplish our wildest dreams.

I have this beautiful photo of a horse that my husband, Mike, and I jokingly call Miss Magistrate because the photo is so large and commanding that she really demands your attention. The photo is beautiful but it sat hidden in my garage for nearly a year. Why? Because it was ruined by the clunky frame it came with.

The photo wasn't the problem, it was everything I wanted for my home, but it needed reframing, literally. It took me a year to figure out just what I wanted it to look like and then find the right frame, but once I did, we hung that photo of Miss Magistrate in our house and she took on a life of her own, free to inspire people with her beauty.

Like that photo, inside of that beautiful body of yours, right at the core, is an even more beautiful soul, filled with courage, bravery, resilience, and love. But it's not always easy to view ourselves that way. Instead, sometimes the "frame" that we hang around our life's story comes from things we tell ourselves like, *You'd be pretty if you lost some weight, You're too afraid to actually do this, You're a failure, You're not allowed to get angry, just go along with things*, or my most used word weapon of choice, *You're completely powerless, and your voice isn't important.*

Have you ever had any of those thoughts? You're not alone. And the good news is you can change your thoughts by reframing them. I stumbled across the following reframing exercise when I was struggling to find a way out of the negative self-talk that was keeping me back from pursuing my purpose. I'm not going to lie, it wasn't easy to untangle these negative thoughts I've had for so long, but when I started practicing reframing my thoughts, I suddenly had the mental energy and mind-set to start pursuing my goals.

How do we reframe our thoughts so that we can reframe how we view ourselves? First, we must tackle the thoughts head on. Acknowledge them, become aware that they are there, and then make a plan to get into a pattern of reframing them. Let's do this together.

List All Your Thoughts

Before we get started, I want you to know that this exercise might feel scary or overwhelming at first, but that's okay. It's a sign that you're doing this right!

First, make a list of all the thoughts that you find yourself thinking throughout the day using the columns on the following page. As the day progresses, keep this book nearby, or jot down in a journal or even the notes app on your phone as these thoughts arise, and then input them into the following page. You might find that you write down the same thought multiple times—that's okay too! We're gathering data right now, and it's all useful.

When you write down your negative thought, take a few moments to think of and then write down a powerful, positive thought that you want to have instead. I write my thought down in the moment I have it, because it helps me notice how many negative thought patterns I'm having throughout the day, and it helps me become more mindful of holding myself accountable for my thoughts. If you're having trouble coming up with a positive thought (believe me, this can be the hardest part of this exercise), think about what you need to hear in that moment. Is it something comforting? Is it something empowering? Channel what your most supportive friend would say to you in this moment, or even what you would say to a friend who is going through this.

For example, when I have the thought, *I am powerless*, I write it down in the left column, then write down this positive thought I can replace it with in the right column: *Thank you, thought, for trying to protect me. But I've got this. I am brave. I am so incredibly brave.* Or when I start a new project, sometimes this thought pops into my head: *What am I doing? I don't know how to begin a new project and I'm too overwhelmed!* (left column). Over time, I've taught myself to think this thought instead: *I have everything I need. I am enough. I have enough* (right column).

Thoughts I Am Thinking:	*Thoughts I Can Think Instead:*

The first several times you replace your negative thought with a powerful one, it might feel really uncomfortable. In fact, you might not believe the new thought to be true for one second! But if we allow ourselves to give so much weight to our negative thoughts, can we, for a moment, learn to allow ourselves to give as much weight to our powerful, positive thoughts?

I wish I could say when you're done with this exercise, you will have mastered those negative thoughts for good. Unfortunately, it's something we all struggle with on a daily basis, but the great news is that once you are aware, you'll start to notice the negative thoughts before they can take hold and can more quickly dismiss and replace them. Once you have control of your thoughts, you'll be surprised how much easier it becomes to work toward the dreams in your life.

Remember, if life was going to break you, it would have already broken you by now. Which means you must be a pretty awesome bada** (I'm trying to refrain from swearing, so bada** will have to do!), so let's learn to think those types of thoughts about ourselves. If we can feel powerful and that we have everything we need in our present moment, then we will have more confidence in what our future holds. Our life becomes what we say it will become, and it starts with our thoughts.

The Five Daily Questions

—and—

Establishing a Morning Practice

The Five Daily Questions

After we've worked to replace the negative self-talk with messages that are true about who we are, it's time to uncover who we are and what drives us. The best way I have found to do that is with a daily practice that includes asking five questions:

1. What is my intention?

2. Why am I worthy?

3. Who can I serve?

4. What can I set down?

5. Who is the truest version of myself today?

I originally uncovered this practice during one of the lowest moments of my life. I went on a discovery journey to figure out what it was that I actually wanted out of my life and started getting really honest with myself about what I needed to let go of. Part of letting go was finding acceptance with my current reality, and allowing myself to be here, in this moment of my life. The reality was that the life I had originally dreamed of having had just been pulled out from under me; I was heartbroken and hardly functioning, and I needed to recalibrate.

I decided that to start, to really get back to who I was, I had to operate from a place of being proactive instead of reactive. It was an overwhelming realization to admit that I didn't know who I was anymore. If you find yourself in a similar space, I'm going to tell you a little secret: it's okay if you feel like you don't know who you are right now, because actually, you do know. You know who you are, you've just buried her. Underneath trying to please other people, or running around taking care of every other human on planet Earth but yourself, or trying to fill the voids you feel is a woman who wants to be seen. Your true self hasn't gone anywhere; she just needs permission to come out again. We're going to do that, together.

As I embarked on this journey of unearthing my true self, the first thing I realized was that I needed to create confidence and space for my own dreams before I consumed others' opinions about what I should be doing. There were *so* many opinions swirling around me: business advisers told me how I should run my business, people I followed on social media told me how I should be dressing, decorating, and eating, and I realized that before noon every day, I would be so buried in other people's ideas or expectations of me, I didn't even know what it was that I wanted for myself. So I started with one rule that changed my life and will change yours too, if you let it:

Create before you consume.

This means that in the mornings, before you check your email, or get on social media to see what everyone else is doing, or get caught up in anything that is going to start sucking your energy for the day, sit with yourself, get quiet, and journal. Dream for yourself. And in that dreaming, in that morning time dedicated to creation and un-covering of who you are, you'll find the space to explore the preceding five questions.

In the next section, I'll give you a thirty-day practice that you can work through each day, asking yourself these five questions and reflecting on what the answers tell you about who you are and what you want to be. These questions can be done in just a few minutes, or you can spend longer unpacking them. Whatever that individual day needs is exactly right. Before you get going, let's spend a minute understanding each question and how it can impact your life.

1. What is my intention?

You might have heard this word thrown around a lot, and if it sounds like some woo-woo jargon, just stick with me for a second! An inten-tion is simply a guiding principle that allows you to stay on course. It's like your North Star. You can set an intention for any part of your life: how you want to feel, what the purpose of a meeting is, what dinnertime at your home will be like—anything!

In the daily practice, the purpose of your intention each day is to create a focus that brings purpose and fulfillment into that day. It can be anything from wanting to show up as a big ball of love with everyone you interact with, to giving your work presentation with confidence, to trying a new recipe. An intention focuses in on the one thing you want to accomplish that day, just one thing, and then allows you to make choices throughout the day that keep you on a clear path, instead of being pulled a million directions by everyone and everything else. This is the starting place for the day.

One note: when we get to the Clarity Mapping section, we'll zoom the lens out further and set a "life intention." I find doing these smaller, daily intentions is both good practice for setting the larger one, and important to ground you in each day.

2. Why am I worthy?

As you start setting an intention each morning and then following through with it, you might start to notice that it feels really uncomfortable! At this very moment, you might be asking yourself, "How can I possibly experience peace and joy when I feel unworthy?" Sometimes, we find comfort in the feelings that we're used to feeling: being let down, sad, and overwhelmed. In a strange way, it might even feel safe there, because it's what we know.

If you're experiencing this (and even if you're not!), try asking yourself this question every morning to get even more clear in your purpose: "Why am I worthy?" Go even deeper and explore: "Why am I worthy of this intention today. Why am I worthy to be here, to feel joy, to continue to grow and step into my power and have clarity in my life?" Unpacking this will be one of the hardest, but also most empowering steps in your journey. The more we accept that we're worthy of the life we want, the easier it becomes to stop sabotaging our lives.

3. Who can I serve?

If the last two questions have been focused on us—who we are and what we want—I've learned that when we are intentional about seeing needs outside of our own, we open ourselves up to be placed in the path of those who need what we can give. When you're called upon to meet another person's need, it creates a feeling that doesn't come any other way.

In a world that is so self-focused, being a leader who looks out for other people is what truly changes the world. Get intentional each morning and ask yourself, "Who can I serve today?" You'll be surprised at how it clarifies what your purpose is.

4. What can I set down?

If we're not careful, our motivation can be drained by guilt, shame, experiences, and thoughts that we don't even realize we're still carrying with us. Asking ourselves this question, "What can I set down?" allows us to pause and consider what isn't serving us anymore on our path to clarity, and to then let it go.

This question came to me a couple of months into my new daily practice. I was making forward movement, I was learning how to be more intentional with my time and choosing who and what filled my life, but I still felt really heavy. I realized I was still giving power to situations and people in my life that I allowed to hurt me over and over again because I kept carrying the weight of the negativity and pain with me, and it was time to set them down.

My first step was getting crystal clear on what I needed to set down. To help myself identify what it was, I did a mental inventory of situations, relationships, or events that were weighing on me and that I had no control over in the present moment. For example, there was an eighteen-month time period where I was having multiple doctor appointments every week. Each appointment gave me an incredible amount of fear and anxiety, and I would spend my days trying to mentally prepare for the next doctor's visit. It was consuming every aspect of my life, and I felt completely out of control because of the unknown variables in my health. I knew I couldn't change the circumstance, but I felt like I could take back control over the power it had over me. Creating a daily practice where I acknowledged the fear my situation was causing me, and then creating permission for myself to take control of my feelings and intentionally strive to create peace in my life, changed my day-to-day anxieties. Once I finally accepted what I needed to set down and took action, I immediately felt lighter.

Setting down what no longer serves you is a gift. And it frees up space for whatever comes your way next.

How do I be the truest version of myself when it's

5. Who is the truest version of myself today?

wanting to ~~show~~ move to fast and the abandonment that comes

Showing up as the truest version of ourselves is the bravest thing we can do. The truest version of yourself might make some people mad. You might have to reevaluate some relationships, and that's okay. It's okay because the truest version of you is finally being given space to fly, and that's the biggest gift you can give yourself.

This question was the missing puzzle piece of what I needed to focus on every day. At first I phrased this question: "How do I show up as the best version of myself today?" But I quickly realized that my best is going to be different for everyone I interact with. We shouldn't have to feel like we should show up one way to one group of people and then show up differently for another because of their expectations of you.

Instead, this question became: "Who is the truest version of myself today?" If you stay true to yourself, no matter how hard it gets or who you disappoint, you can hold your head high in knowing that you are no longer burying the brave girl who lives inside of you.

Establishing a Morning Practice

C reating your own morning ritual is the most important first step to getting really clear about your intentions and aligning yourself and your goals with the life you want to lead. I'm so excited for you to cultivate your own practice! Doing this in the morning allows you to start the day with the cleanest slate possible and it's easier to keep everything else that's vying for your attention at bay. That said, the most important thing is that you're making space to get intentional. If you find that the afternoon or evening is the best for you to do that, that works too!

To help you establish a successful morning practice, I wanted to share some guidelines I've found to be helpful:

1 **Create time for your practice.** Listen, I get it! You have kids who wake up at the crack of dawn to watch cartoons, you can barely find clean underwear each morning, you have a project due that currently has dog hair all over it, a demanding boss, an early morning Peloton ride that's hard enough to get out of bed for . . . there are a million reasons *not* to create time. And here's where your two choices come back into play: run from your pain or reclaim your power. And I know you chose option two because you're still here with me, so let's create a plan right now so that you're not left grasping for more minutes in the day, and then the first thing to go is your practice.

Can we start by committing to just five minutes? More time will become available throughout the weeks you spend doing this, because you're going to be getting really clear on other things that need to fall away in your life, but right now, we just need five minutes. Allow that five minutes to become a nonnegotiable. If you're stressed about how to fit in five minutes with everything else you have going on, a reframing thought could be, "I am deserving of clarity, joy, and freedom in my life. And it comes five minutes at a time."

2 **Create a physical space for your practice.** Finding physical space to do this practice in is incredibly important! When your morning practice feels special, you'll receive more clarity and focus while you spend time there each morning. You can find a space in the corner of your room, in your office, in your closet . . . anywhere that you can dedicate to being still. This is a place dedicated to *you.*

In this space, hang a small piece of art that inspires you, a quote that pumps you up, your affirmations, and maybe even the five questions that you will be going through every morning. Sometimes I light a candle so the room smells fresh, and other times I sit on my yoga mat. Set an intention that this space is for your growth, your clarity, and your freedom.

3 **Create consistency in your practice.** Starting a new routine can feel like someone is pulling out your teeth. Have you ever tried to start a new habit, perhaps working out or cutting down on sugar, and experienced how nearly impossible it felt at first, but easier as you showed up each day? As you continue your morning practice, it will get easier and become something that you actually look forward to because of how good it makes you feel. But to get there, it requires you to do the work. Consistently showing up for yourself is the work that you're being called to do right now.

4 **Create community in your practice.** Finding even just one person who is on this journey with you, or with whom you can have accountability, can be the difference between you abandoning all of it or completely changing your life. It's also helpful to have a friend you can check in with. Let your significant other, your mom, your book club, or someone you really trust know what you're doing and that you'd like to check in with them. You might even invite them to do it with you! Of course I hope that you join our online community; you can find me on Instagram @AshleyKLemieux and I am always here, on this journey with you.

5 **Create emotional space to reflect on your practice.** At the end of every week, use this statement to look back on the work you've done the last seven days, and give yourself credit for doing it: "This week, I affirm . . ." Take time to notice the hard steps you've taken, take inventory of feelings you've had and progress you've made, and encourage yourself that you're on the right path. We can get so caught up in trying to get somewhere that we don't notice what's happening in the actual process of getting there.

By doing this morning practice for thirty days, which I'll walk you through in the next section, you will have developed a pattern of clarity that will aid you in creating your Clarity Map. Your Clarity Map will empower you to move forward with intention, offer tangible action steps to bring a dream to life, and give you guidance to know what to focus on in your life. You're building something amazing: your real, truest life. Let's get going.

SECTION THREE

Thirty
Days to Clarity
and Freedom

Here's where we put your morning practice into action!
Spend at least five minutes every morning asking yourself these
questions and recording the answers. Remember, it might feel hard
or uncomfortable at first, but by the end of the thirty days, you'll
wonder how you ever started your day without it!

Day 1

1. What is my intention?

To create peace in myself in good
and hard situation

2. Why am I worthy?

3. Who can I serve?

4. What can I set down?

5. Who is the truest version of myself today?

_____

_____

_____

Journal prompt: What do I fear? Take a moment and think about what need might be behind that fear and write it down.

_____

_____

_____

_____

_____

_____

_____

_____

_____

_____

_____

_____

_____

_____

_____

_____

_____

_____

Day 2

1. What is my intention?

_____
_____
_____

2. Why am I worthy?

_____
_____
_____

3. Who can I serve?

_____
_____
_____

4. What can I set down?

_____
_____
_____

5. Who is the truest version of myself today?

_____

_____

_____

Journal Prompt: What feelings do I want validated today? What feelings do I have today that are asking to be validated? For example, I might feel overwhelmed with all the tasks I'm trying to complete and people I'm trying to care for throughout my day. Validating that feeling and then identifying what can help hold space for that can add moments of clarity and calm that I'm needing. Maybe it's as simple as a five-minute walk alone, or taking a bath after the kids are in bed. Or perhaps I'm really excited about an accomplishment and I want to validate my hard work and celebrate. When we pay attention to our feelings, it allows us to be more intentional with holding space for ourselves and what it is that we need, so that we don't get lost in the shuffle of our own lives.

_____

_____

_____

_____

_____

_____

_____

_____

_____

Day 3

1. What is my intention?

_____
_____
_____

2. Why am I worthy?

_____
_____
_____

3. Who can I serve?

_____
_____
_____

4. What can I set down?

_____
_____
_____

5. Who is the truest version of myself today?

_____

_____

_____

Journal Prompt: What if failure is really time and space for growth? What is one thing that I would do if I wasn't afraid to fail?

_____

_____

_____

_____

_____

_____

_____

_____

_____

_____

_____

_____

_____

_____

_____

_____

Day 4

1. What is my intention?

_____
_____
_____

2. Why am I worthy?

_____
_____
_____

3. Who can I serve?

_____
_____
_____

4. What can I set down?

_____
_____
_____

5. Who is the truest version of myself today?

_____

_____

_____

Journal Prompt: When have I experienced a failure that led me to something fulfilling and new?

_____

_____

_____

_____

_____

_____

_____

_____

_____

_____

_____

_____

_____

_____

_____

_____

_____

Day 5

1. What is my intention?

_____

_____

_____

2. Why am I worthy?

_____

_____

_____

3. Who can I serve?

_____

_____

_____

4. What can I set down?

_____

_____

_____

5. Who is the truest version of myself today?

_____

_____

_____

Journal prompt: How could I view past failures as experiences that led to growth? How does that change my willingness to try something new or different?

_____

_____

_____

_____

_____

_____

_____

_____

_____

_____

_____

_____

_____

_____

_____

Day 6

1. What is my intention?

_____
_____
_____

2. Why am I worthy?

_____
_____
_____

3. Who can I serve?

_____
_____
_____

4. What can I set down?

_____
_____
_____

5. Who is the truest version of myself today?

_____

_____

_____

Journal prompt: Take a moment to think about the past week and anything that happened that may have felt like a failure. What did I learn from it? What are some ways I can apply this to next week/going forward?

_____

_____

_____

_____

_____

_____

_____

_____

_____

_____

_____

_____

_____

_____

Day 7

1. What is my intention?

2. Why am I worthy?

3. Who can I serve?

4. What can I set down?

5. Who is the truest version of myself today?

_____

_____

_____

Journal prompt: **This week, I affirm:**

My need to . . .

_____

My goal of . . .

_____

My ability to . . .

_____

My work in . . .

_____

My hope for . . .

_____

Myself

Day 8

1. What is my intention?

_____
_____
_____

2. Why am I worthy?

_____
_____
_____

3. Who can I serve?

_____
_____
_____

4. What can I set down?

_____
_____
_____

5. Who is the truest version of myself today?

_____

_____

_____

Journal prompt: When is a time where I felt let down by someone else or maybe even by myself? How would forgiveness set me free?

_____

_____

_____

_____

_____

_____

_____

_____

_____

_____

_____

_____

_____

_____

_____

_____

_____

_____

Day 9

1. What is my intention?

_____
_____
_____

2. Why am I worthy?

_____
_____
_____

3. Who can I serve?

_____
_____
_____

4. What can I set down?

_____
_____
_____

5. Who is the truest version of myself today?

_____

_____

_____

Journal prompt: Is there anyone in my life I want to forgive? If I could, what would I say to them?

_____

_____

_____

_____

_____

_____

_____

_____

_____

_____

_____

_____

_____

_____

_____

_____

_____

_____

Day 10

1. What is my intention?

_____
_____
_____

2. Why am I worthy?

_____
_____
_____

3. Who can I serve?

_____
_____
_____

4. What can I set down?

_____
_____
_____

5. Who is the truest version of myself today?

_____

_____

_____

Journal Prompt: What would forgiving myself feel like? What would I need to hear or know to truly forgive? Start writing a letter to yourself below:

_____

_____

_____

_____

_____

_____

_____

_____

_____

_____

_____

_____

_____

_____

_____

_____

_____

_____

Day 11

1. What is my intention?

_____
_____
_____

2. Why am I worthy?

_____
_____
_____

3. Who can I serve?

_____
_____
_____

4. What can I set down?

_____
_____
_____

5. Who is the truest version of myself today?

_____

_____

_____

Journal prompt: What is something I'm proud of myself for?

_____

_____

_____

_____

_____

_____

_____

_____

_____

_____

_____

_____

_____

_____

_____

_____

_____

_____

_____

Day 12

1. What is my intention?

_____

_____

_____

2. Why am I worthy?

_____

_____

_____

3. Who can I serve?

_____

_____

_____

4. What can I set down?

_____

_____

_____

5. Who is the truest version of myself today?

_____

_____

_____

Journal prompt: What does love feel like? How can I create that feeling today?

_____

_____

_____

_____

_____

_____

_____

_____

_____

_____

_____

_____

_____

_____

_____

_____

_____

_____

Day 13

1. What is my intention?

_____

_____

_____

2. Why am I worthy?

_____

_____

_____

3. Who can I serve?

_____

_____

_____

4. What can I set down?

_____

_____

_____

5. Who is the truest version of myself today?

_____

_____

_____

Journal Prompt: What do I love about myself?

_____

_____

_____

_____

_____

_____

_____

_____

_____

_____

_____

_____

_____

_____

_____

_____

_____

Day 14

1. What is my intention?

_____
_____
_____

2. Why am I worthy?

_____
_____
_____

3. Who can I serve?

_____
_____
_____

4. What can I set down?

_____
_____
_____

5. Who is the truest version of myself today?

_____

_____

_____

Journal prompt: This week, I affirm:

My need to . . .

_____

My goal of . . .

_____

My ability to . . .

_____

My work in . . .

_____

My hope for . . .

_____

Myself

Day 15

1. What is my intention?

_____

_____

_____

2. Why am I worthy?

_____

_____

_____

3. Who can I serve?

_____

_____

_____

4. What can I set down?

_____

_____

_____

5. Who is the truest version of myself today?

_____

_____

_____

Journal prompt: What do I want to feel today? What do I need to do to feel that?

_____

_____

_____

_____

_____

_____

_____

_____

_____

_____

_____

_____

_____

_____

_____

_____

_____

_____

Day 16

1. What is my intention?

_____
_____
_____

2. Why am I worthy?

_____
_____
_____

3. Who can I serve?

_____
_____
_____

4. What can I set down?

_____
_____
_____

5. Who is the truest version of myself today?

_____

_____

_____

Journal prompt: What is one action my future self would thank me for taking today?

_____

_____

_____

_____

_____

_____

_____

_____

_____

_____

_____

_____

_____

_____

_____

_____

_____

_____

Day 17

1. What is my intention?

_____
_____
_____

2. Why am I worthy?

_____
_____
_____

3. Who can I serve?

_____
_____
_____

4. What can I set down?

_____
_____
_____

5. Who is the truest version of myself today?

_____

_____

_____

Journal Prompt: Why is it okay for me to feel happy today?

_____

_____

_____

_____

_____

_____

_____

_____

_____

_____

_____

_____

_____

_____

_____

_____

_____

Day 18

1. What is my intention?

2. Why am I worthy?

3. Who can I serve?

4. What can I set down?

5. Who is the truest version of myself today?

_____

_____

_____

Journal prompt: Why would I still be worthy of love, joy, and peace, even if today doesn't go according to plan? It's easy to only feel deserving of these things once we think we've "earned" them or proven ourselves. But my individual self-worth is an inherent truth that can't be altered or taken away. I don't have to keep trying to prove my worthiness of being loved.

_____

_____

_____

_____

_____

_____

_____

_____

_____

_____

_____

_____

_____

_____

_____

Day 19

1. What is my intention?

_____
_____
_____

2. Why am I worthy?

_____
_____
_____

3. Who can I serve?

_____
_____
_____

4. What can I set down?

_____
_____
_____

5. Who is the truest version of myself today?

_____

_____

_____

Journal prompt: What are some ways I can talk to myself today to remember my worthiness?

_____

_____

_____

_____

_____

_____

_____

_____

_____

_____

_____

_____

_____

_____

_____

_____

_____

Day 20

1. What is my intention?

2. Why am I worthy?

3. Who can I serve?

4. What can I set down?

5. Who is the truest version of myself today?

_____

_____

_____

Journal Prompt: How can I connect to my higher power today to remember that I am loved?

_____

_____

_____

_____

_____

_____

_____

_____

_____

_____

_____

_____

_____

_____

_____

_____

_____

Day 21

1. What is my intention?

_____
_____
_____

2. Why am I worthy?

_____
_____
_____

3. Who can I serve?

_____
_____
_____

4. What can I set down?

_____
_____
_____

5. Who is the truest version of myself today?

_____

_____

_____

Journal Prompt: This week, I affirm:

My need to . . .

_____

My goal of . . .

_____

My ability to . . .

_____

My work in . . .

_____

My hope for . . .

_____

Myself

Day 22

1. What is my intention?

_____
_____
_____

2. Why am I worthy?

_____
_____
_____

3. Who can I serve?

_____
_____
_____

4. What can I set down?

_____
_____
_____

5. Who is the truest version of myself today?

_____

_____

_____

Journal prompt: What is something new I can try this week that will bring me joy?

_____

_____

_____

_____

_____

_____

_____

_____

_____

_____

_____

_____

_____

_____

_____

_____

_____

_____

Day 23

1. What is my intention?

_____
_____
_____

2. Why am I worthy?

_____
_____
_____

3. Who can I serve?

_____
_____
_____

4. What can I set down?

_____
_____
_____

5. Who is the truest version of myself today?

_____

_____

_____

Journal prompt: Where am I the happiest in my skin and spirit?
This can be a physical or emotional place, or both!

_____

_____

_____

_____

_____

_____

_____

_____

_____

_____

_____

_____

_____

_____

_____

_____

_____

_____

_____

Day 24

1. What is my intention?

_____
_____
_____

2. Why am I worthy?

_____
_____
_____

3. Who can I serve?

_____
_____
_____

4. What can I set down?

_____
_____
_____

5. Who is the truest version of myself today?

_____

_____

_____

Journal Prompt: Why does it feel scary to be true to who I am sometimes?

_____

_____

_____

_____

_____

_____

_____

_____

_____

_____

_____

_____

_____

_____

_____

_____

_____

Day 25

1. What is my intention?

_____
_____
_____

2. Why am I worthy?

_____
_____
_____

3. Who can I serve?

_____
_____
_____

4. What can I set down?

_____
_____
_____

5. Who is the truest version of myself today?

_____

_____

_____

Journal Prompt: **How will I stay connected to my power today?**

_____

_____

_____

_____

_____

_____

_____

_____

_____

_____

_____

_____

_____

_____

_____

_____

_____

_____

Day 26

1. What is my intention?

_____
_____
_____

2. Why am I worthy?

_____
_____
_____

3. Who can I serve?

_____
_____
_____

4. What can I set down?

_____
_____
_____

5. Who is the truest version of myself today?

_____

_____

_____

Journal prompt: What if I need nothing else today except everything I already have inside? It is easy to see what other people have, or spend three minutes on social media and walk away feeling like we're falling short and need a million things to be better or to catch up. What if I'm worthy, just the way I am, in this moment?

_____

_____

_____

_____

_____

_____

_____

_____

_____

_____

_____

_____

_____

_____

_____

Day 27

1. What is my intention?

_____
_____
_____

2. Why am I worthy?

_____
_____
_____

3. Who can I serve?

_____
_____
_____

4. What can I set down?

_____
_____
_____

5. Who is the truest version of myself today?

_____
_____
_____

Journal prompt: What are some of my gifts or qualities I feel especially proud of in myself? How could I use my gifts to create change in someone else's life?

_____
_____
_____
_____
_____
_____
_____
_____
_____
_____
_____
_____
_____
_____
_____
_____

Day 28

1. What is my intention?

_____
_____
_____

2. Why am I worthy?

_____
_____
_____

3. Who can I serve?

_____
_____
_____

4. What can I set down?

_____
_____
_____

5. Who is the truest version of myself today?

_____

_____

_____

Journal Prompt: This week, I affirm:

My need to . . .

_____

My goal of . . .

_____

My ability to . . .

_____

My work in . . .

_____

My hope for . . .

_____

Myself

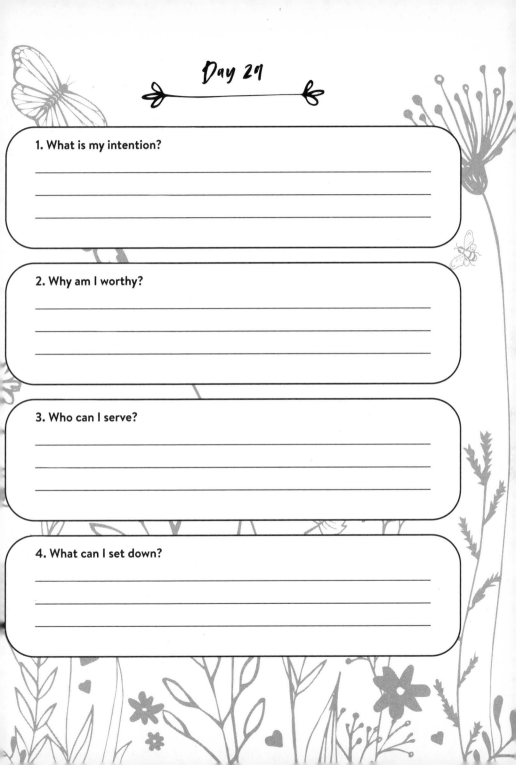

Day 29

1. What is my intention?

2. Why am I worthy?

3. Who can I serve?

4. What can I set down?

5. Who is the truest version of myself today?

_____

_____

_____

Journal prompt: Who am I? Who am I, really?

_____

_____

_____

_____

_____

_____

_____

_____

_____

_____

_____

_____

_____

_____

_____

_____

_____

_____

Day 30

1. What is my intention?

_____
_____
_____

2. Why am I worthy?

_____
_____
_____

3. Who can I serve?

_____
_____
_____

4. What can I set down?

_____
_____
_____

5. Who is the truest version of myself today?

_____

_____

_____

Journal prompt: What am I ready to go do that I was not ready for thirty days ago?

_____

_____

_____

_____

_____

_____

_____

_____

_____

_____

_____

_____

_____

_____

_____

_____

_____

*C*ongrats—you just accomplished the first thirty days of your new practice of intentionally creating clarity every day. I wish I could hug you in person, so consider this a giant squeeze from me . . . unless you're more introverted and would hate that, then an air five will do!

Let's take a deep, deep breath here. You just stayed committed to thirty days of intentional living. Despite everything going on around you and perhaps thoughts that were happening inside of you, you pressed forward and created an empowering moment of clarity that helped guide your path for the last month. You might have had some breakthroughs, perhaps you trust your intuition now more than you did before, maybe you worked through a fear that's been holding you back for a long time, or perhaps you feel lighter after setting some things down that are no longer serving you. Maybe it was one big moment of clarity that you experienced, or perhaps it was subtle changes each day that built up to something greater. Sometimes even just faithfully showing up to do the work is enough. The beauty of creating space for clarity in our lives is that once we understand that we have the ability to operate from a place of being proactive about what happens in our lives instead of constantly reacting to the things that happen to us, little by little our lives build up to be what we want them to be. You're back in the driver's seat, my friend!

Doing this clarity practice every morning helps me become aware of what is happening around me, inside of me, and to me. I lived on autopilot for so long that, at first, actually taking moments to notice how I felt, to ask myself important questions like how I was really doing that day, to take time to unpack what thoughts or things I needed to let go of in my life was really exhausting and hard. It felt like waking up, and you might feel yourself waking up again too. It's exciting and terrifying all at once, and I want you to know that both feelings are okay. Once I started to give myself permission to feel whatever feelings I had that day, then I gave myself permission to process through them and stop trying to keep stuffing them into the dark cracks inside of me.

When you live your life awake, you live in the light. You live free because your ability to make the best decisions for your life is empowered by healthy processing and thoughts instead of decisions that are driven by fear and being overwhelmed. And here you are, awake and ready to live your life, just by creating space for a simple, daily practice.

How Do I Know If Any of This Is Working?

Now that you've started this new practice, you may be wondering if anything is really changing. Remember, you're just starting out on this journey, and we are all beginners at some point. I LOVE being a beginner. It feels new, exciting, and fresh. The opportunities at the beginning are endless, as we are about to discover new feelings and ideas we've never had before. I also understand that beginning something new can be deeply overwhelming. And that's okay. When I am overwhelmed, I reframe my thought to be something like, "I am excited for the new opportunities coming my way." Sometimes overwhelm and excitement can feel similar.

You are here because you've listened to an inner push that something needs to change, that you want to create a life you absolutely love, and that you are ready to do it. When you commit yourself to your morning practice, you're proving to yourself that you will not settle for anything less than clarity, freedom, and possibility in your life and that you're putting in the work so that you will find it.

You'll know the process is working when you have moments each morning where new ideas come to your mind. Those ideas will start to create a path for you, which will then produce positive feelings that you might have been searching for your entire life. When you begin to feel peace and clarity in your life, first in little moments and then more and more frequently, you will know it's working. Even if everything feels like it hasn't quite come together yet and you're still doing a lot of uncovering, that feeling of peace never lies to us. It doesn't lie to us because there's no other worldly feeling that can mimic it. Look for peace. When you feel peace, allow it to be confirmation that you have taken another step in the right direction.

It took me a while to see a huge difference in my life; because so many small changes were happening, they didn't hit me all at once. But looking back, as you complete these pages and are able to see what you've written on Day 1, and then where you are on Day 30, you will be able to track your progress and see how far you've come in just thirty days. But remember, this is a no-pressure situation. There are no expectations that need to be met other than to show up. This is working when you begin to trust yourself, your feelings, and the work that you were born to do in this world. I don't know about you, but I can't wait to see you step more fully into who you are, because the world needs more women who are confident in their value and worthiness.

✶　　✶　　✶

With your head feeling a little clearer and your heart a bit more ready, it's time to dive in to creating your very own Clarity Map. This map will be a companion throughout your life, a tool you can come back to over and over to help you make the small and large decisions in your life. Whether you need help making a big professional pivot or are seeking more fulfillment in your home life, Clarity Mapping is the tool to help you continue to uncover your path and then experience tangible results.

Reimagine Your Future with Clarity Mapping

Through reframing your thoughts, establishing an intentional morning practice, and asking yourself five important questions each day, you've taken large, brave steps to create forward momentum in your life. Now it's time to figure out where you want that momentum to take you. We'll do that with Clarity Mapping, a tool that will help you channel that momentum you're experiencing into a simple, actionable, and authentic direction. This tool helps you identify your purpose and plot out your path.

I created Clarity Mapping after I spent several months in my new morning practice. I felt that I had made progress on uncovering who I was and I was ready to figure out where I wanted to go. Using it, I went from someone overwhelmed by life to someone overjoyed by it.

Clarity Mapping is the pinnacle practice of this workbook. It's the five questions working together to uncover the larger answer to how to live a meaningful life. It has changed my life and the lives of countless other women just like you. Some people have told me how they've started new businesses that once felt incredibly out of reach. Others have uncovered more confidence and have clearer direction on how and where they should be spending their precious time. Many have told me that Clarity Mapping has allowed them to get more done in four weeks than they normally would do in an entire year. It opens the gateway to a clear, focused mind.

Brainstorm Your Life Intention

You just created thirty daily intentions as you moved through your clarity practice, which prepared you for what we'll do next. It's now time to create your main life intention to help you figure out your next steps. A life intention can look like "I create peace and love in all that I do," it can look like "I empower women to uncover their power," or it can even look like "I intentionally build a home of safety and hope for all who enter." Now, for some of you, I can already hear the pressure you feel to make the one right choice! This is a no-pressure situation; your intention can be changed at any time. Try something out, if it works, great; if it doesn't, you have all the power and flexibility to try something else.

My hunch is there is something that you *know* you want. The clearer we get, the clearer your life will become. Jot down a few possible intentions that come to mind here:

1 _____

2 _____

3 _____

Here are traits your intention needs to have to make it the most impactful:

1 Specific: The more focused the intention, the easier it will be to live out. For example, if you're leaning toward, "I want to be a good mother," explore what being a good mother looks like to you. Perhaps your intuition is telling you that you want to be more present in your family life. What does that look like? Maybe being present means less screen time for everyone or managing schedules better so there's more quality time together. An example of your new, specific intention might be:

"I create an intentional family life by prioritizing our relationships and increasing the time we spend together."

Remember, if you get stuck, keep digging deep, keep asking why this intention is important to you. Keep asking yourself "why" until you run out of whys, until all that's left is deep, inexplicable desire.

2 Measurable: Evaluating your progress can be difficult, which is why I always recommend starting off with a measurable goal. For example, "I want to be my own boss/start my own business" or "I want to be a good mom" is beautiful and noble, but it doesn't give you a tangible way to assess your growth. In the revised intention above, you can easily keep track of how much time you're spending with family. You can see if progress is being made, and if it's not, you now know which part isn't working that you need to tweak or rework.

3 Positive: Since our intentions are often rooted in our problems, it's easy for negativity to creep in and I'm not here for it, not one bit.

"I want to be a good mom" implies that you're a less than wonderful parent. This exercise is not meant to beat you down; it's about building you up. Just like we reframed negative thoughts into positive ones in the first section, make sure your intention is framed positively by centering the positive result you want from your intention. Again, the revised version is a positive reframing of this: "I create an intentional family life by prioritizing our relationships and increasing the time we spend together."

Aim and Action

If you're feeling stuck here, I want to share with you what I call my Aim and Action exercise. There are two questions that you can ask yourself to help narrow down your intention:

1 "How do I want to FEEL right now in my life?" This is the aim. Allow yourself to really lean in to what feeling you're craving to feel. Maybe it's more peace, love, joy, security, safety, success . . . or something else! Understanding what your intuition is desiring to feel will give you your aim.

2 "What do I need to DO to feel that?" This will help you determine the action you need to take. If you feel overwhelmed and panicked most days but you want to feel peace, what is the first thing that comes to mind that you know you need to do to help cultivate that positive feeling? Use the columns below to work through current ideas:

Aim:	*Action:*

Let's take a minute and brainstorm some ideas for intentions that are specific, measurable, and actionable. Use the space below to jot down as many ideas as you want.

_____

_____

_____

_____

_____

From the collection of ideas above, what most resonates with you right now? Does one of them light a fire in your soul or feel like it gives you that peace we've been talking about? Choose that and write your intention smack-dab in the middle of this box:

Here's where I'm going to break you into two groups. You can join both groups if you want to, but I really want to focus what I'm about to say to make it as specific, and therefore useful, as possible.

If the intention you wrote in your box has to do with your personal growth, relationships, home, spiritual life, or anything of this nature, keep reading the next section. These pages will be focused on personal clarity and growth.

If your intention has to do with career, business, or entrepreneurial endeavors, then I will see you on page 116. I will be centering those pages for you specifically for business clarity and growth.

Again, you may want to create a Clarity Map for both your personal and your professional life. Great! Think for a moment about which area of your life feels like it could use the most direction and start there.

Personal, Relationship, Home, or Spiritual Life Clarity Map

1. Choosing Your Intention

On the next page you will find the entire Clarity Map. We're going to walk through one box at a time to build it all out. The box in the middle is where you are going to rewrite your intention. I wanted you to write it twice because if it didn't feel like it was *the* one when you committed to it the first time, you now have an opportunity to change it, to go deeper if you need to, to let go of any fear that is telling you that intention feels too scary, and go all in with me right now. The boxes surrounding where you are going to write your intention are how we are going to bring your intention to life!

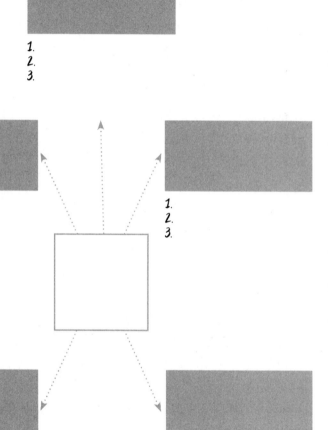

1.
2.
3.

1.
2.
3.

1.
2.
3.

1.
2.
3.

1.
2.
3.

As you look at your intention, alone there in the middle of your paper, we're going to pause to do a reframing thoughts exercise. I want you to make a list of every single thought that's coming up right now when you think about that intention in the left column:

Thoughts I Am Thinking:	*Thoughts I Can Think Instead:*

Do any of these thoughts sound negative or need reframing? Is your mind trying to tell you this process is going to be too hard? Is there some forgiveness that needs to happen or are there boundaries that need to be established in a relationship? If thinking about actually doing these things makes you want to run and hide, it's okay to acknowledge that. Maybe bringing your intention to fruition is going to require some difficult and honest conversations. Maybe the conversation is even with yourself.

Let's use the sample intention from the last exercise—"I create an intentional family life by prioritizing our relationships and increas-

ing the time we spend together"—so you can see me work through a
Clarity Map while you build out your own. I originally set this intention right after we lost our kids and our marriage was floundering
(honestly, this tool is one of the ways we saved our marriage after our
loss that made us forget what our relationship could be!). When I set
it, I remember feeling like nothing was going to help Mike and me
come back together powerfully, and I was too tired to try. I would try
to convince myself that we were grieving, so therefore our marriage
was just going to suffer, or that we spent enough time together since
we both worked from home, even though it was not intentional or
quality, or that it would be easier to do our own separate things under
the same roof. The pain of acknowledging that family life now only
consisted of the two of us instead of the four of us made it all brutally
impossible. Or so I thought. One thought at a time, I had to shift
my thinking about each negative thought pattern I told myself and
create a new, truer one that wasn't led by fear or habits that had been
chaining me down for a long time.

Since you've gotten so good at reframing your thoughts, you are going to do that right now with the lies your brain is trying to convince
you are true. Next to any negative thoughts you wrote down in the
left column, write a positive thought to replace it in the right column.
Once you've finished writing down a positive thought for each negative thought, read the positive thought out loud to yourself. Let's create
new thought patterns to help your intention be able to come to life.

2. Tackling Mental Roadblocks

This next part is fun because it really helps bring everything full circle. This step continues to push down mental roadblocks that may arise and gives you space to work through anything left that you need to work through. Armed with answers, now we continue to fill out the boxes.

You know how you just spent thirty days answering five questions? You will answer the questions again, but this time, answer specifically pertaining to the intention that you have in the middle of your box. Look at the intention in the box. Ask yourself:

1 What is my intention? Well, this should be easy!

2 Why am I worthy? Why are you worthy of this particular intention?

3 Who can I serve? What ways does this intention allow you to serve someone else? If your intention is around your own personal or spiritual growth, that is equally important. Sometimes, the person you need to serve right now is yourself.

4 What can I set down? What are the obstacles that might be keeping you from being able to achieve this intention?

5 Who is the truest version of myself as I work to bring my intention to life? Jot down what this version of yourself looks like.

3. Taking Action

As you look at the Clarity Map, you will see empty boxes surrounding your intention. We are going to fill these with action steps, but first let's brainstorm what those steps might be. Remember the Aim and Action work you did a few pages ago? Go through the actions that you initially wrote and, with your intention in mind, write down any other actions that would help bring your intention to life. It doesn't matter if you know how to accomplish it yet or not; what's important here is that you list out all the actions that you know are required to get your desired result.

Actions:

_____

_____

_____

_____

_____

_____

_____

This work you're doing here is about to come in handy! Look at the list of actions you've written down, and now circle the five that you can start doing right away and that will create the most momentum for you.

Write your narrowed-down list of five actions here:

1 _____
2 _____
3 _____
4 _____
5 _____

These five actions will each go in their own box on your Clarity Map. We will develop each action further, but look at you, you're making major progress!

Using my example, "I create an intentional family life by prioritizing our relationships and increasing the time we spend together," here are the five action items I will use to fill in my Clarity Map on the next page.

1 *Nightly family dinners* _____

2 *Phones away after 5 pm* _____

3 *Talk about our feelings together* _____

4 *Cut out harmful distractions* _____

5 *Do a hobby together* _____

Nightly family dinners

1.
2.
3.

Talk about our feelings together

1.
2.
3.

Phones away after 5PM

1.
2.
3.

I create an intentional family life by prioritizing our relationships and increasing the time we spend together

Cut out harmful distractions

1.
2.
3.

Do a hobby together

1.
2.
3.

Now, choose one action box to focus on. I will choose "Cut out harmful distractions" for this example. For the action you've chosen, make a list of the things you need to do to make that happen. I find a list of about three to five items to be best. My list looks like:

1 *Limit screen time to one hour a day.*

2 *Keep out media and songs that don't invite feelings of peace into our home.*

3 *Come up with alternatives to do together instead of screen time—maybe card games would be fun?*

4 *Set boundaries on work hours so we can have quality time together.*

5 *Reevaluate friendships or people that are causing stress in our lives.*

Looking at your list, you will now circle the top three things you can do first. To evaluate where to start, answer the following questions:

Is it motivating?

Is it meaningful?

Is it manageable?

List the three steps that you chose underneath your action in the numbered list. Now, you will repeat this step for all five of your actions that are on your Clarity Map! Look at this beautiful, intentional life you've just created. You've gone from feeling overwhelmed to carving out your own path forward.

This Clarity Mapping practice can be a guide for you for the rest of your life. You can come back to it when you need to reevaluate, at the start of each year when you have new dreams to reach, at times when you feel you're at a crossroads and don't know what choice to make; this map is a tool to help you lean more fully into the one person you can always trust: yourself.

I'll see you in Section Five, on page 133, to take our final step together of reclaiming your power.

Career, Business, or Entrepreneurial Clarity Maps

1. Choosing Your Intention

For those of you whose intentions are focused on their career and business right now, it is great to see you here. The work I've done with business owners and those wanting to take their professional lives to the next level is some of my most favorite work! I started my company with $300, basically our entire savings, in a cockroach-infested condo as a new college grad and built it to what it is today. Though it might sound like a linear process, most of the time it doesn't work out that way. It has taken me going back to the drawing board time and time again. What it boils down to is making the most out of the resources that I have, instead of focusing on what I lack, and really figuring out what direction I want to lead in that is true to who I am, regardless of what other people want from me. At one point, I even let go of a seven-figure company because it created a life of stress and overwhelm that I just could not live in anymore. My advisers, friends, everyone really, thought I was absolutely crazy and tried to offer me different solutions. For over two years I tried and tested their solutions, but in my gut, I knew what I needed to do. Once I started trusting myself more, I started being able to make confident decisions that, although hard at the time, have led me down a path of fulfillment, success, joy, and creating that I otherwise would have never uncovered.

You might be here right now because you find yourself in the same situation. Perhaps your business takes so much energy from you every day that you have nothing left to do the one thing that made you begin your business in the first place.

Or perhaps you want to start a new business and have no idea where to start, with very few resources and many fears that you're going to fail before you even try.

Maybe you're not an entrepreneur, but you're so unfulfilled in your current job that you have no desire to get up and drive to work every day, and you don't care if you never see your boss again. You have passion and drive but it feels stagnant and you just can't live one more day on the hamster wheel that's taking you nowhere.

Do you fit any of these? If you do, you're in good company. The really exciting news is that there's a way forward into a brighter, bolder, more enjoyable future in your professional career. We need to do some heavy lifting to get in motion, but I promise you, it will be worth it.

Before we dive in, I want to tell you that every experience, every crappy job or "failed" product launch, every passed-over promotion or financial investment lost has led you to this very moment. Where you are right now has been your training ground for where you are headed. Don't discredit all you've done to get here, because even the jobs that feel like they've sucked the life out of you have been guide-posts in your life, signaling to you to get back on your path, gently reminding you that you are called for something more. Something more fulfilling, purposeful, and life-giving.

I'm going to ask you a question right now, and I don't want you to think too hard about it. I want you to literally write down the very first thing that comes into your mind:

What do you *really* want out of your career?

_____

_____

_____

Why do you want that?

_____

_____

_____

Okay, now I'm going to ask you again. Why do you want that?

_____

_____

_____

And again. Dig deeper. Is there a reason beneath the ones you gave above? Why do you want that?

_____

_____

_____

One last time. Really get real with yourself. Why do you want that?

_____

_____

_____

How will you feel if your career brings you that?

_____

_____

_____

That feeling, that desire, it's real. It's possible. The reason behind what we want out of our business and career is a very powerful motivator that is driving us. Just now, you went five layers deeper to really think about why this is all so important to you. That driving force that you uncovered at the root of your deepest needs and desires? Let that be the reason that you continue to do this work. Let that push you when the mountain feels too high to climb. You can do hard things, and when you know there's something greater leading you forward, you can do impossible things. If you are seeking a dream that might feel impossible, it means it's available to you because your inner intuition is telling you that it's out there waiting for you! Now it's your job to do the work and then see what happens.

Let's get working on your professional Clarity Map, and it starts with the foundational piece: your intention. After I started my morning practice and took some big leaps to shift who and what was allowed into my life, my life's intention became very clear to me:

"I guide women to uncover their power."

I wrote that in the middle box of my Clarity Map. On page 123 is your Clarity Map. The middle box is where you are going to write your intention. Let's start by giving you some space to brainstorm what your intention might be. Use the lines below to write down any and all ideas that come to mind—no one else will see this, so don't worry about bad ideas!

_____

_____

_____

For each of these intentions, I want you to write "I" in front of it. The more concise your statement is, the easier it is going to be for you, and others, to clearly understand what it is that you are trying to build. If you're stuck trying to reframe your intention so that it can start with "I," a good pattern to follow is:

What do I do?

Who do I do it for?

What is the result?

When I answered these questions as I came up with my own intention, it looked like this:

What do I do? I guide people. I've always felt it is my purpose in life to help guide others through the hard stuff they face that makes them feel stuck because I know what it feels like.

Who do I do it for? I do it for women like me. Women who don't know what to do next. Women who have so much passion and purpose burning inside of them, but might need help reigniting their spark because it's been blown out along the way.

What is the result? The result of guiding women is it allows them to uncover their power. They step into it. They remember who they are and who they were always created to be.

In every project I take on, in everything I write, in every keynote I give, and in every intention I set, I follow the pattern of: "What do I do?," "Who do I do it for?," and "What is the result?" Using this framework will help you unlock a lot of clarity. In fact, let's have you answer those questions right now:

What do I do?

_____

_____

_____

Who do I do it for?

_____

_____

_____

What is the result?

_____

_____

_____

What did that exercise uncover for you? Did it lead you to narrow down your list of intentions? Let's choose one to use in the Clarity Map. Remember, you aren't committed to this—if you get going on the map and it doesn't feel right, you can always choose another.

Now we're ready to write our intention in our Clarity Map. In the middle box on the map below, write your intention.

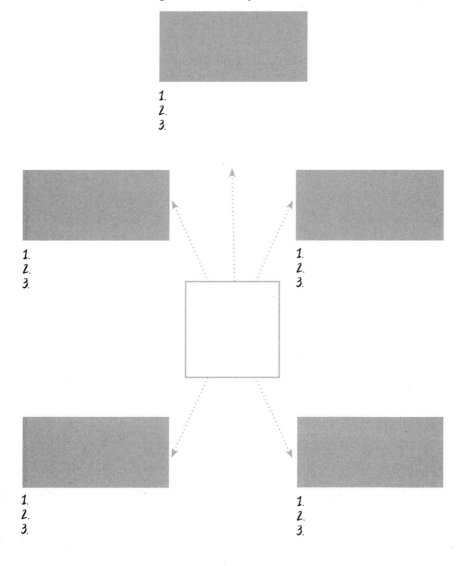

It gives me chills just thinking about those beautiful, guiding words that you've done SO much work to uncover! Look at the progress you've already made; it feels really good to get clear, doesn't it?

Okay, now we are going to figure out everything that needs to happen so that what is in your middle box becomes a reality. As you look at your intention, alone there in the middle of your paper, I want you to make a list of every single thought that needs reframing right now. What is coming up in your mind that might be causing some fear or apprehension? Are you worried pursuing this is going to be too hard, or you don't have enough money to make it happen, or are you telling yourself you're not qualified enough? What are the things that your mind is trying to tell you will be roadblocks to bring this to life? I have found that, often, bringing our intention to fruition requires some difficult and honest conversations, starting with ourselves.

When I first set my intention, I had just been turned down by every major publisher I had sent my first book proposal to. You want to talk about fear and failure and not feeling qualified to do the work I felt called to do? Those rejections played over and over in my mind, leading me to start rejecting myself, my truth, who I was. But do you want to know what my why was? After digging deeper in the five layers exercise, I found my why is because I didn't want anybody to feel like I did. And maybe, just maybe, the work that I do will also someday reach my two children who are out there in the world, helping guide them to continue to uncover their power and feel freedom and clarity in who they are. Because of that, I knew that I had to keep going.

One by one, I had to shift my thinking about each negative thought pattern I told myself and create a new, truer one that wasn't led by fear or habits that had been chaining me down for a long time. Since you've gotten so good at reframing your thoughts, you are going to do that right now with the lies your brain is trying to convince you are true. Let's create new thought patterns to help your intention come to life.

Thoughts I Am Thinking:	*Thoughts I Can Think Instead:*

2. Tackling Mental Roadblocks

Here's where everything comes full circle. This step helps bring more clarity, continues to push down mental roadblocks that may arise, and gives you space to work through anything left that you need to work through. Armed with answers, now we continue to fill out the boxes.

You know how you just spent thirty days answering five questions? You will answer the questions again, but this time, specifically pertaining to the intention that you have in the middle of your box. Look at the intention in the box. Ask yourself:

1 What is my intention? Well, this should be easy!

2 Why am I worthy? Why are you worthy of this particular intention or professional achievement?

3 Who can I serve? What ways does this intention allow you to serve someone else?

4 What can I set down? What are the obstacles that might be keeping you from being able to achieve this intention?

5 Who is the truest version of myself as I work to bring my intention to life? Jot down what this version of yourself looks like.

3. Taking Action

As you look at your Clarity Map, you will see empty boxes surrounding your intention. We are going to fill these with action steps, but first let's brainstorm what those steps might be. Remember the Aim and Action work you did on page 105? Go through the actions that you initially wrote and, with your intention in mind, write down any other actions that would help bring your intention to life. It doesn't matter if you know how to accomplish it yet or not; what's important here is that you list out all the actions that you know are required to get your desired result.

Actions:

_____

_____

_____

_____

_____

This work you're doing here is about to come in handy! Look at the list of actions you've written down, and now circle the five that you can start doing right away that will create the most momentum for you.

Write your narrowed-down list of five actions here:

1 _____

2 _____

3 _____

4 _____

5 _____

Those five actions are now what you fill the boxes surrounding your intention with! Pretty cool, right? My five actions were:

1 *Write books.* _____

2 *Host in-person retreats.* _____

3 *Create accessible online workshops.* _____

4 *Launch a podcast.*

5 *Create videos for social media that women can relate to.*

Each action item I chose was a way for me to reach out to the women I wanted to serve, a way for me to begin living out my intention. The actions you select don't have to be grand gestures; they can be small, meaningful steps that make sense for you and your life. The goal is to create forward motion, not to overwhelm you by thinking you need to win first place in a marathon that you've never run before.

Now, you are going to choose one action to start with. I will use "write books" as this example. I started making a list of everything I needed to do in order to write books:

1 *Write a book proposal—Need to research what this looks like.*

2 *Send it to literary agents, or pray that one finds me! Will ask friends for introductions.*

3 *Set aside six weeks where I go all in in writing my book— Find out when I can schedule. Produce a book tour that creates powerful moments of courage for the women who attend.*

Do this for all of your action items, and so your filled-out map will look similar to my example on the next page:

Write books

1. Write a book proposal
2. Send book to literary agents
3. Set aside six weeks where I go all in writing my book

Create videos for social media that women can relate to

1. Turn speaking engagement footage into videos
2. Learn how to add captions to videos to make them accessible for everyone to watch
3. Choose one day a week to dedicate to video creation so that I'm never left scrambling

Host in-person retreats

1. Decide what topics would benefit my audience most
2. Map out each retreat day
3. Secure venue and date

I guide women to help uncover their power

Launch a podcast

1. Create podcast name and topics based on needs I see online
2. Find podcast editor so I'm not overwhelmed
3. Confirm first five guests and record

Create accessible online workshops

1. Identify what my audience wants the most in help and community
2. Dedicate one week to filming and content creation
3. Set up a launch team

Make a list of the steps that need to be taken to bring your first action item to life here:

1 _____

2 _____

3 _____

4 _____

5 _____

Now, looking at your list, circle the top three items that will allow you to get started right away and make a big impact. When I choose my starting place, I ask myself these three questions:

Is it motivating?

Is it meaningful?

Is it manageable?

Take your top three actions and put them under your main action. Do this for every action that you have on your Clarity Map. Looking at your map, you now have five very tangible, mapped-out actions that are going to bring your intention to life. I focus on one to three actions at a time, depending how in-depth they are. And then, step by step, I see my dream come to life.

Now it's your turn. You've worked hard and sifted through so much to get really clear, to claim what it is that you want out of this life and the time you've been given. Now it's time to claim what was always meant to be yours.

Something that's helpful for me is to create a timeline that holds me accountable and gives me a clear boundary of what I'm committing myself to. As you look at your actions, the next step is to set realistic timelines for each one. I like to create space for myself in between the due dates I give myself so that I don't get overwhelmed. Next to each action, write the dates you will both start and then complete them by. This will help to not leave your forward movement feeling open-ended.

This Clarity Mapping practice can be a guide for you for the rest of your life with any intention you want to welcome into it. You can come back to it when you need to reevaluate, at the start of each year when you have new dreams to reach, at times when you feel you're at a crossroads and don't know what choice to make; this map is a tool to help you lean more fully into the one person you can always trust: yourself.

SECTION FIVE

Reclaim Your Power

The most powerful part about this process of digging deep within ourselves is that as we figure out where it is that we want to go, we also figure out who it is that we want to *be*. On our journey to go somewhere, we also *become* someone. Someone who is full of bravery and passion and light and love that otherwise might not be there if we weren't choosing to live this life awake and free.

Just because you're moving down a path of clarity and freedom doesn't mean you won't experience hard things again. In fact, I've come to realize that it's quite the opposite. When you stop running away from hard feelings and situations and confront them, it means that there will continue to be more uncomfortable moments in your life. I don't say this to scare you, but to prepare you. So that you know when resistance comes, it's not some sign to call it quits, but an opportunity to dig deep again into the power that you hold. Those moments are what create the beauty and intentionality of your life.

Reclaiming your power isn't about eliminating pain; it's understanding that though pain may be a part of your experience, it isn't a part of your identity. After Clarity Mapping became a part of my practice, I spent a long time wondering how I would sustain forward momentum when life got tough. The key for me when it came to maintenance was less about where I wanted to go and more about who I wanted to be when I got there. Through the work you've done in these pages reframing your thoughts and Clarity Mapping, you've discovered that many of the answers you seek are already inside you. I shared my path, but you have uncovered your own. Take a moment to let that victory sink in. I hope you're as proud of you as I am.

Reflection Activity

Take a deep breath and close your eyes. Keep breathing as you imagine you've just accomplished your intention—it can be years from now or even tomorrow, depending on your intention. Picture who the people are that you want to be surrounding you, notice what you are doing and what you look like.

What does it feel like in your body to have accomplished this intention? What about your soul? What are the physical and emotional sensations?

Open your eyes and write down exactly how it felt in the space below:

_____

_____

_____

_____

_____

_____

_____

_____

_____

_____

_____

_____

You've reframed your thoughts, you've reimagined your future, and now you reclaim your power. What needs reclaiming in your life? To identify that, we first start with identifying things that maybe we've given our power away to. Giving your power away means that you've given somebody, something, or some memory the ability to speak, act, or think for you. It could be that a feeling of stress arises any time you log into your bank account because money has been given your power. Or maybe it's hard for you to use your voice because situations in the past have led you to believe that it is easier to stay quiet. Maybe there is someone who has deeply hurt you, and holding on to the resentment toward them is keeping you from living out of your power. Whatever it may be, the great news is that you can take your power back. The journaling activity on the next few pages will help you identify what's draining your power and give you some tools for how to protect it.

Protecting-Your-Power
Journal Activity

What Drains My Power?

What things, people, or experiences have a pattern of taking my power?

What is the thing that, if I let it, would keep chipping away at my worth and how I feel about myself?

What is the thing that binds me down, that makes me forget who I am and where I'm going?

How do I currently feel when I think about these experiences?

Rewrite My Story

How would I *like* to feel when thinking about these experiences?

What is the main thing in my life that I want to reclaim?

Replenish My Power

What things, people, or types of experiences inspire me or replenish my energy?

How can I cultivate these relationships or dedicate time to these activities?

What needs to be set down in order to dedicate more time to cultivating my replenishing relationships or dedicate more time to positive activities?

Schedule Time To Replenish Myself

Write down a date/time/day of the week that I know that I have time (be honest with myself!) and commit to doing that activity, no excuses.

Activity:	Date:

Did you write about a relationship, a thought about yourself, or a habit? Maybe it was a fear, a memory that has chained you to the past for years. It's okay to see it staring back at you. It's okay because the power doesn't belong to it any longer.

The power belongs to you. And right now you are choosing to take your power back from it by not allowing it to control how you view yourself and the world anymore.

Discovering Your Personal Affirmation

Using what you just wrote down, we are going to create a personalized affirmation. Its purpose is to provide power and encouragement and to recenter your mind on the truth of who you are when you need to be reminded. You can create affirmations in several ways, but I love creating them as "I Am" statements. For our purposes, this affirmation is going to be an "I Am" statement that brings all your power back into exactly who you are and want to be.

As you look at what needs reclaiming, what is the word that came to mind when you thought about how you *want* to feel? Write that word down.

_____

For example, in the spring of 2020, my body unexpectedly went septic while sixteen weeks pregnant. Within hours I went from healthy and hiking in my backyard to being rushed to the hospital and almost losing my life. As a result of the sepsis, I lost our baby boy a couple of days after being admitted to the hospital. Everything felt scary after that. Every ache in my body, every muscle twitch or headache—I didn't know if I was okay, or if I was going to be on the verge of death. The amount of medical trauma that I went through made me feel very unsafe in my own body. I gave my power away to my fear that at any moment, I would literally just drop dead and there would be nothing I could do about it. The fear paralyzed me for a while. I knew that I had given my power away to my sepsis, and I was too scared to take it back. When looking at that experience, I know that what I want to feel in my life is safe. I have "I am safe" written in so many places around my house they've become a permanent fixture. I verbally remind myself and my body, every single day, that I am safe.

"I am safe" has become a very important affirmation to me. It is the exact opposite of how I initially felt after going septic, and as I've declared "I am safe" every day for months, an amazing thing has happened. I feel safe now. I've done the work to get to a place of being able to trust my body again, of relearning how to evaluate if I need quick medical attention, and taking my power back because I know that I can trust myself.

Now it's your turn. Think about what you want your affirmation to be. What is a need that comes up frequently for you, maybe when you're stressed or down and out? Maybe it's even something that you wrote down in the List All Your Thoughts exercise. What is that thing you want to feel? Jot your thoughts down in the space below; these elements will help you craft your affirmation.

_____

_____

_____

_____

_____

_____

_____

_____

_____

_____

_____

_____

Take a look at the words above and try blending them together in a beautiful, simple sentence that states exactly what you want. This can be a statement like "I am safe" or a fact like "I have everything I need." Your affirmation will help you reclaim your power.

Next, write your finished affirmation on a paper and stick it everywhere you need to so it continuously reminds you of the power that you hold. In fact, here's a page that you can write it on and tear out of the book to use.

✳   ✳   ✳

Whenever you feel yourself slowing down, I want you to remember six affirmations that will help reignite your power. I wrote about these six "I Am" affirmations in *I Am Here*, because they declare what is true about you, and you can claim them. These are mantras that have changed my life, and you can adapt them as your own, change them, or use them to get ideas for new mantras that will guide you in the future. They are:

I AM a Fighter

I AM Loud

I AM Not Alone

I AM Safe

I AM the Rainbow

I AM Free

You are on the top of your mountain; don't be afraid to shout it! The affirmations I've chosen are precious to me. I've whispered them and I've yelled them. I've written them on sticky notes and emailed them to myself. When I get down about everything I'm not, they remind me of everything I AM. Take them and remember that you ARE, too.

I AM
A FIGHTER

I AM LOUD

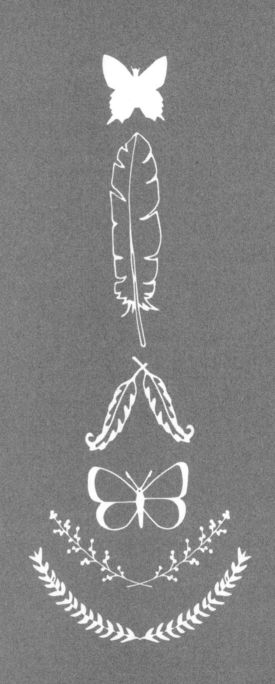

I AM

THE

RAINBOW

i am
FREE

CONCLUSION

Moving Forward

In the very beginning of this workbook, you answered the question, "What am I ready to do?" Look at everything you've done during our time together. You're not merely ready to do it anymore; it is now a reality. You've turned failures into lessons, pain into power, and being stuck into clarity. You've actually *done* it, and this feeling, this moment of accomplishment, can be a pattern that holds strong in your life, over and over again.

So where do you go from here? You keep moving forward. You continue to reframe your thoughts when old patterns creep in, you spend time reimagining your future as often as necessary so that you uncover your clear path forward, and you keep reclaiming your power. Sometimes we view reaching dreams or big life milestones such as graduating from college, getting married, having kids, or landing the job as the end result. And then when we arrive at a place where we've reached that end result or something happens in our lives and takes away the thing we dreamed of for so long, it feels like the end. But it's not the end, it's the beginning. It's the beginning of a new opportunity, a new way of living, a new chance to discover who we are in that season. Once I stopped viewing both my dreams and my painful moments as the "end goal" or "end reality," I stopped feeling so stuck when I found myself there. Your new skill of Clarity Mapping will continue to show you what opportunities are out there waiting for you. You're never actually stuck. As you've seen through this process, who you are deep inside is always there, pressing and calling you to a path of fulfillment.

Everything in your life has led you to this moment. You are here. With your past, present, and future supporting every step of the way. I want you to affirm all the work that you've done. Let yourself feel proud. What has this time uncovering your path meant to you? We will finish our time together with your words to yourself. And remember, this isn't the end. This is your new beginning.